lamping wild rabbits

Simon Maddrell

Out-Spoken Press
London

Published by Out-Spoken Press,
PO Box 78744
London, N11 9FG

A CIP record for this title is available from the British Library.

First edition published 2026
ISBN: 978-1-0686712-9-6

Typeset in Futura and Adobe Caslon
Design by Patricia Ferguson
Printed and bound by Print Resources

Out-Spoken Press is supported using public funding by the National Lottery through Arts Council England.

LOTTERY FUNDED
Supported using public funding by
ARTS COUNCIL ENGLAND

lamping wild rabbits

CONTENTS

caged rabbits

feral rabbits

dungeness rabbits

wild rabbits

dead rabbits

*

it’s as though
we have to climb
out of our damage
up an invisible rope
and apologise.
a rope we’ve been carrying
all our life
dangerous
swings as a kid
when a cord snapped
a lasso in a cowboy dream
maybe a tug-of-war between
the blues and the pinks
or dragging a fire truck
away with our teeth
rope in a stone dungeon
blindfolded in a dark
room
there is a thing
unspeakable hiding inside
my liver
it hides
anywhere
in the body
we imagine
it
hanging from a rope
which we’ll call
fear
for want of knowing
any other
choice

caged rabbits

[gripped]

father's [

[   ] straight

]

]

[   ] smudge

where [

]

[   ] hidden

[ ] semen-stained [

]

[   ] awakenings

[   ] stay [

in nineteen ninety-one i stepped out of my skin

for the first time there was a young man
sucking a cock like he'd arrived back home
at last —

not in the sense of the seventies
oblong blocks of *manx ices*, unwrapped
shoved into a round cone

but more so that rocket lolly
you remember, wide at the bottom
ridged with a sweet-lipped tip.

the nineties wonder at what dialling
0898 offered — cool, fresh & wild for it
until just after that moment of melting white

hundreds & thousands flashed by
— now too exposed to survive so raw
i crawled back into my skin, sagging

dragging itself to the bathroom
where i threw up.

the boy [erased]

didn't want to be different

but [

]

]

[ ] leaves [ ] sickness

no medicine [

]

[ ] it was [

[ ] a secret [

i woke [

[ ] guessed

]

such [ ] strange

fancies [ ] thoughts

bluespine unicornfish

two tail-held scalpels
like its surgeon sisters
white meat with pink tinges
a set of grey scales
like its unicorn brothers
an obvious protrusion
with unknown purpose
one blunt kitchen knife

& when i cut i cut open
the bone to blame
the blood for what it is

wound paint

splashed over the whole
body with special attention

all organs are sensitive
even karma has limits

irreverent jokes about sacral
chakras, kumquats in the mouth

peeled-back physalis, the juice
sharp-tongued fossils in resin

felled trees my desires
wounds painted videne

you didn't care whether pinky & perky

were boys or girls until they were
two albino rabbits going to market
in those days difference had a value
bilberries or blackberries filling up
an eight-gallon jam pan a clock
to measure the time to go home
while most parents used the sun

when you played in the woods
you'd hesitate with rope swings
thinking they'd snap but all you
ever did was fall though you didn't
tip out of that rowing boat while
wearing a life jacket or off rocks

at grandpa's fishing school —
bamboo rods in a tiny cove with
fish so stupid you'd never eat them
unlike the crabs with a different hook
you never mastered the deftness
to tickle trout as if subtlety is art
you can only admire.

albino

I thought Pinky & Perky had been stolen though
my brother showed me a place in the woods
where he said our rabbits were hanged. Fifty
years later my sister tells me they were eaten
by a fox while we visited Blackpool Illuminations.

Do parents make up a tolerance ranking for children
to face? I only ask because Father said he'd prefer
a thief to a queer for a son. No wonder I was petrified
by my own mortality — after Grandma died
they decided not to tell me she had been stolen
or even eaten by a fox.

Albinos are a natural occurrence but under certain
conditions they do not survive long. I wonder
if all this is connected to the obsession I had with
my *Palomino* sweatshirt — recognisable only
by the branded label against the back of my neck.

how i once loved the bedtime cocoa ritual

milk slowly frothing in the pan, the heart-shape in its
middle refusing to bubble. Off the stove shushed
quickly poured into the gloopy mess.
I could never stir the lumps out of it like I could with
custard, like I did with custard every Sunday.
It wasn't custard that was banned.

Plastic sheet, two gauze metal mats — cloth taped to
the edges to stop the hurting as if I wasn't enough
already. Thick cotton under nylon so I wouldn't feel
like an experiment, abandoned later, because I was.
Crocodile clips wired to a big metal box

my Mickey Mouse clock blocked. Big switch,
big red light, big bell inside. When I woke up
it already happened.

a small grey bear soaked in piss

taught me the difference between giving
& being given, keeping it clasped
for far too long… the doctor said
he should have outgrown it by now.

I used to hide treasure in a bed
of forget-me-nots. An oil drum
produced forced rhubarb giving
early crumbles & pies —
it turns pinker, sweeter, more tender.

Dad stealing peat from Bolton moors
taught me the difference between
taking & being taken, his spade cut it
into pieces to feed his strawberry bed
it retains moisture and aids growth.

on port erin beach in 1970

My elder brothers are trying to drop my hand-me-down
trunks green with loose elastic. Paul tries to jump on top
of me as we run around a deep hole dug by their two
metal spades and mine of hollow yellow plastic.

I smash it across his temple then the end turns red.
I jump to the bottom of the pit hoping for the tide
to come in. The agreed family solution is to refill the hole.
No-one wants to be buried alive.

Paul's future is shrouded in 1990 after diving off the wrong
side of a weir. He's broken his neck. In hospital his arms
are strapped onto splints like a cross with a tube down
his throat.

You see the cross isn't to crush his breath, as in a crucifixion
but to stop Paul pulling out the pipe and trying to escape.
This time, I jump on top of him in the same bed where
his lungs drown a week later.

As with the scar I left him, I still don't know if I regret it.

treehouse

i.m. Paul Douglas Maddrell [1960-1990]

My brother built a treehouse as a kid, fifty-foot up an old beech
in the woods next to my big school, years before I learnt
anything there. He coaxed me to climb it — the silver-grey
bark hard & slippy — I was a shaking leaf, like many boys
in my brother's presence.

He climbed ahead like a cat, not a leopard with its prey
but with a nonchalant faith its kin would follow.
I can't remember what was in the treehouse.
At the big school next to the woods, I'd tell classmates
my brother built 'that' —

Twenty-odd years later, after he died, I searched for the
treehouse and found remnants still hanging, my brother left
in the arms of a trunk — I'm certain my brother carved
hard into the bark, and even though I couldn't recognise which
it was about a girl.

nature poem

after Danez Smith

the leaves have flounced their annual fall
the branches skeleton the sky with an odd
fruit. i didn't want to start with leaves
adorning the silver birch

i love how they fade to yellow triangles
with a sunset-pink. no-one wants to read
a poem about nature, much prefer
the nature of our bodies

something easy to blame, bodies cut
at the wrists and bleeding out. how leaves
fall to the ground, bury themselves, rot
in layers like shame

see how easy it is to mention shame?
is it possible to ban shame even from
a gay boy's poem? I walk in the woods
thinking of how the purity of silver-barked

youth peels daily from its trunk like tissues
how i used to pick at it and gently stroke its skin
how their smooth twigs age and develop warts
there i go again talking about shame

how the bark matures too and develops dark
soil on a gay boy's shoulders. hanging. there i go
again talking about our dead, and if they are not
your dead, you are lost to the nature of being

our language drips

Our native   Yn Ghaelg
was nearly silenced from what
only it   can express.

I nearly zipped   my own life
in a black-bagged lack   of understanding
that it is language   that restores our place

that speaks louder than any plinth
that   when it cries   deepens the sea.
It is near impossible   to describe the sun

to feel its language   forming a new dark.

stones in his pockets

i.m. j.h

she asks about what i have lost
— *i haven't even found it yet*
i reply, skeeting the rocky beach
to pocket pebbles of hexes &
witches

unanswered, holey stones hanging
from branches, threaded like seeds
of queer-shaped fruit like Jarman's
films i live with squandered
spirals

a pub chat and threads missed
i imagine it was like being hanged
but without his neck breaking
who knew what he meant by —
i'm going for a swim

even a stone has a soft spot

a worn-through hole after years
of attrition, a heart whose emptiness
is its strength

a mill grinds wheat and a cup fills
how their threaded weight makes
looms and fishing nets complete

and if by chance, you don't
believe in hexes, hold one stone
with one hole, in one hand

notice if your eye resists a telling
stare, drawn through by its own
event horizon, like the heart pulls

your dark blood then blows out bright

the snow leopard bites its own tail

i.m. c.f.

but no-one knows why... the source of warmth
appears an enemy   she sees   what I don't
from that mountain ridge   and feels it more
deeply hunting blue sheep in a herd of wild
ibex

she lost a cub — a choice that wasn't — both
too young to fend for themselves — she lost a
child and took me to a play about AIDS.
she survived on thin air but no-one knows —
how rosettes camouflage dark spots

floating on flurried lakes — a father raged
his violent storms leaving him alone she
nourished three children through peaks
and vales she never would roar beyond.
the captive live longer than the wild —

notions etched in unbearable visibleness —
when the snow melted   she bit her tail
once too often no-one knows why   chemicals
ferment an imperfect storm-blinded terrain
where escape is as high as you jump.

according to locals

a twelve-year-old boy was kidnapped
by four men in Kenya. One week later
while the police were chasing the kidnappers
the kidnappers were chased by three lions.
The three lions saved the boy. Then the police
saved the boy by chasing the three lions
who would have eaten the boy once he had
stopped crying. Which just goes to show how fine
the line between living & dying is.

Meanwhile, the youngest-ever Samaritan volunteer
wanted to kill himself. All because a Bible preached
that his body was off-cut meat. His thirst was so great
that he supported one million people in Kenya
to build their own dams, an approach that, according
to locals, is called mwethya.

Then he saw, face to face, that the crucifix in his eye
was only dust.

1 queerinthians 13

after 1 Corinthians 13: 1-13

11 When I was a child, I thought as a child, I understood
as a child, but when I became a man, I could not put
away my shame.

13 Three things remained: love, hope, shame, these three.
The greatest of these was shame.

4 Shame is a darkness with no darker shadow
it does not envy, does not puff up, is not proud.

6 Queers do not behave unseemly but do seek their own.
7 We believe it all, hope it all, bear it all, endure it all.

12 Looking in a mirror with no light, I saw face to face,
then shame to shame. I let myself through this dark
glass and knew in part, now I know. That love is love.

1 If I kiss the tongues of men & angels and have joy,
then I am unabashed brass, a clear & potent cymbal.

the [erased] faggot

trusted [ ]

[ ]

not even time

]

]

]

fears

]

]

healing [

[ ] cutting [

]

[

[ ] telling

]

[ ] forgets

]

]

a golden wedding

after Essex Hemphill

they don't know we are becoming powerful. every
ring we place on a cock belongs each *time*
we milk our seed we heal our sickness, *we*
whisper new   we vow to *kiss*
horsemen naked not wearing hoods *we*
honour our brothers & sisters who *confirm*
and not destroy our blooming honey is *the*
rosebud drawing in light seen & being in a *new*
media era knowing we now belong in the *world*
free loving queers with a dream still *coming*

according to the signs

The footpath to Port y Vullen is not passable at high water.

My mind floods and races with anticipation
I circle the sea-walled Raad ny Foillan passing
under a civil war battery like we face in our own
islands, the unoccupied land where I find a tiny
bathing creek

— looking purpose-made for the likes of us —
private and delicious like the young men I imagine
in this cove, a secret space to be ourselves with carc
less abandon and timely attention to all the tides
flowing inside, even rippling in our depths one
could be left alone with

the only escape being those uphill trails towards
Gob ny Rona — paths within bracken and woods
a maze hiding many answers — common hornbeam
downy birch, Sitka spruce, crab apple, field maple
even oak from across, a wild cherry with many arms.

the lost [cook]

[   ] shirt [
]
two faces burning [

[   ] hands full [
[   ] thoughts
slipping [

[   ] harder [
]
[   ] tilted [

[   ] he will
[
[   ] wipe the pattern off [

bhadrajun fort

the bedroom door solid
though barely a person
wide enough to fit, unbolted
with a ledge to step over
into the evening sun through
stained glass gecko & spidered
shadows on a throw.

he didn't follow or knock
later, still kept me awake
anyway, many a princess
must have languished
here, their shape still
trapped in the mattress.

good friday

on a rocky shore
gather a flitter or two
with a stick before
they have time to think
sever their muscular feet
discard the black sacs

bake them in their shells
with soddag on a stone
beside a driftwood fire
without nails from a crosh
eat using a cuirn twig
with the thick triangular cake

throw away the remaining
shligganyn out to sea
knowing a flitter is a limpet
like a partner once held
dancing over the embers
with a distinctive stomping step

everything i let go has teeth marks

a parrotfish in the quiet of the night
weaves a web across a crevice
to get some sleep.

during the day it gnaws coral
to death shits out the bone.
skin is the true edge
of my cage.

animals in small pieces

I wish for us to be sponges, masters of self-
recognition with the capacity to restore
damaged parts without conscious thought.
I'd shred & sieve the yellow sponge into
the cloudiness of single cells, chop & repeat
with the cream sponge, blend into a magnolia
soup, leaving both to steep. We'd return to our
separate selves, cling to a rock on a sandy bed,
watch a blacktip reef shark hang in the tide.

feral rabbits

the boy and his arms

after Wilfred Owen

the boy hungers for a bloodletting
tightly drawn from famishing flesh
cartridges empty with steel sharpness
even though they leak blood & meth
he strokes out blind, blunt bullets
and longs to nuzzle the guts of lads

tracked arms show the clawed effects
like tanks bruise battle-zones & homes
fixed eyes swap in a far faraway stare
as pity lurks in curled-up fingers
teeth aren't laughing round an apple
tears sting his burnt cheeks

one size fits all

fuck me again *& i'll buy you a drink*
the best chat-up line you've never had, though
not a pick-up line exactly as *again* suggests
in the dark room at XXL a sexy younger man
i had seen in paradise by the dancefloor light.

it all went prickly pear-shaped
after he moved back with his old boyfriend
a few weeks later the club banned
female hair, make-up & *sequins*
a sequinned masc. hiding a speck of darkness
overcome on a femme boy's face

balls glittered up like a drag queen
we protested in lipstick & lip-synching Cher — they
soon closed it down became Bankside Yards
— a first fossil fuel-free mixed-use facility.

private members' club

he was mouth-opening
beautiful
i couldn't believe my luck
at The Gentlemen Baristas
a Savile Row tailor
lean and neatly cut
i found out later
he wined & dined me
at The Wolseley
all so English-like
he was not
a member
of the private club
like i was
to let him inside later
drank vodka martinis
in a dim-lit corner
kissed in that way
moisture meant desire
he loved rimming
was very persuasive

in the unisex cubicle

did something else

i didn't

say yes then

said no

getting his black cab

he said

you've passed the test!

i found out later

he hadn't

and neither

had i

at the first sex party I go to

I spend the whole time in the kitchen
having arrived with a pocket of rubber

when my assumed one-on-one disappears
to join whatever-number-some play in the lounge.

I am sucked into the kitchen by a naked beauty
party snacks lined-up on a plate on the counter-top

— there are straws for moreish truffling. A perfectly-formed
ass points my way with a comely glance.

I have been fuelled into lesser-resistance, my jean-pockets
stay in the lobby — I gasp & gasp, then gasp — nip back

for the safety in my jeans, returning to gasp until each
& every gasp is empty. Our pillow-less talk has its own

gulps & blows — apparently his ex came with him
for the test, said sorry for leaving it six months —

he's been partying since yesterday since the *yes* —
since the *yes, but don't tell anyone.*

For over forty-eight hours I am numb, don't tell
anyone there, or anywhere else, and even then

it's just A&E, who take a test, and lose it, like I lose it,
like the feeling I am yet to lose, because there is nothing

to lose — yet — until the PEP doesn't work — and then
there is — everything — and nothing works — not blame

— and neither regret.

did he... ?

The sexual health advisor is confused as my unrequited love
quietly shifts his ass in his seat, then makes his excuse to leave
me all alone — in the way that every kind of love is
conditional, in a way that he knew how I felt about him
— for all those years.

The doctor doesn't understand how you got it
despite the lost test, the late PEP and clashing medication
despite the size of someone's viral load. My seroconversion
was perfectly-timed.

The private detective inside me knows
I had a valid test three months earlier, a week before fine
dining at The Wolseley, before the vodka martinis down my
throat, before the incident in the nighttime cubicle.

The private detective disagrees with himself
it's impossible to tell one time from the other
one time is definitely different from the other
it matters and doesn't matter
in that moment
time has no intention
but kills you anyway.

lamping wild rabbits

Chalking gravestones with Dad tracing family logic —
inscribed, fading ancestors, crumbling islands of stone.
Polaroids of people gone, re-faced for posterity,
white-powdered cheeks, dust marks death on my pants.
Both watching gravestones falling out of the colour TV,
tombs advertising AIDS cracking the mantelpiece,
Rock Hudson's *Dynasty* crashing the spotlight,
those disowned corpses engraved nowhere.
Nowhere to hide, like lamping wild rabbits,
headlight executions reflecting my fear
of *myxomatosis* spreading, swollen-eyed deaths
of epidemic proportions discussed in armchairs
with Dad, puffing his care for island burrows.
Ravaging wild rabbits, sea kale desolated
at Prospect Cottage, like Derek. *Sebastiane*
and *Caravaggio* my celluloid palliation in VHS.
HIV — a greater rabbit-shocked fate, but still
my gravestone stands, waiting, chiselled,
painted peacock pink.

i could have been you

i.m. Dursley McLinden (1965-1995)

born just six months later
in the same place,
on the same island.
even though i can't act or sing or dance
but apart from that, we shared
a common fear of cybermen

we couldn't hide behind
the same sofa even though we had that same
difference in our way before *it's a sin* was sung

we tried to escape from shame
i hid in a similar island home,
river-locked in the forest of dean.

even though i was fifteen years behind
your pink-palaced fun and *follies*,
we were both *the man most likely to*

realise our ambitions with *damn*
yankees and a charity to help others.
even though we juggled so much — we cut
friends in half, and we were cut up
too after contracting HIV.

you a *diamond* in the fatal eighties,
even though twenty-five years later for me,
we played around those safe spaces
across from our sexsick island.

even though in the *remembrance of the daleks*
you faced it down, and *phantom*-ed
the opera with ten weeks to live.
i could never have been you
because i used to wish i was dead.

a manx politician walks into a mirrored room

tells himself with a straight face
that revealing the numbers living with HIV
would shed the island in a bad light

like mist after dusk over our mountain
every water drop being an RNA copy
of each clouded figure

the minister transfixed by the medical list —
few gays amongst the fishers & farmers
though all brothers & sisters in blood

needles shadow an infinity of backs
this mirror shows him
with a condition far worse

stigma

means

i have

become

a lethal

secret

weapon

i detest

privacy

terminal illness

elaborately

stops

murders

time

itself

life confirmed as   a time bomb

a poisoned chalice   in a ghetto
a chastity ring   frightened &
three-lettered   unhappy people
long-sleeved   who can't tell the truth
sick-ugly   to others & ourselves
throbbing   my whole body
so well-cloaked   a struggle
if only I knew   how to make life
chosen silence   open & acceptable
sequinned boots   to disclose my secret
awful socks   & survive Margaret Thatcher

dungeness rabbits

in memory of derek jarman (1942–1994)

dungeness

the driest body in england   but the inside
an isolation   full of
sagging shells   oozing
radiation in the bones   dog roses
bleached and skeletal   sea kale
leaves rotted   dried out
sickness blows through me   like tumbleweed

fucking like fairlight donkeys   more a joy than bother
sex kittens still scamper in   my garden
gorse passion   red poppies splash
my body   the landscape
where it remains   rusting chains
a threaded necklace   water to gravel
hanging   dust to wind

powered by HIV

like dungeness
an overactive fuel
energy from atomic
cell destruction

a harsh wind laying
waste its beauty
a fission of dreams
drawings and plain
bloody-minded will

keep on trying
trying to keep on
smiling in slow motion
like those horsemen
riding the tide

famous for fairlight donkeys

a famously brazen film director robbed by time
of today's cinematic freedoms with its own
walls & fences & dances

a garden infused throughout the chelsea shows
from the world's largest shingle beach

Oryctolagus cuniculus, a devil in disguise, neither
whistled nor named, a talismanic doom
for fishermen & their sea kale plots of land

home to a third of Britain's plants amidst
standing stones & dragon's teeth, where duck-
billed dinosaurs grazed & browsed

shores of herbivores i'd never seen — except
for those clapboard cottages & clapboard films

the only imprint from him — for some, maybe
— a stack of pebbles bought from B&Q

for Neil Bartlett

after the bluebells turned to concrete

we turned left into yellow windows
his taste downed the chintz curtains
in dungeness — *the dangerous nose*

could smell its potential gallons
of bitumen paint evaporating in a whiff
just as he wished one day for all his works

the cottage will rot plants shrivel gravel-blind
films self-combust like gorse his signature
on the grave slate will wash, long after this decay

in concrete & radiation he will remain
blue

the visitors

a host of lichens comes
stubble on a rock-hard chest

mosses too, a muted softness
licks, caresses the feet

like in bed after sex
even the rarest of beings

i see them in the wind
i hear fungus in my mouth

crambe maritima

anointed with a necklace of holey
stones and flint from the lowest
tide, a new life for driftwood in
a sea kale spring bloom, till now

a purple bud on a corky stem
protruding pink-edged pebbles
if only this were a metaphor for sex
dying away completely in winter

death has a sticky honey scent
but grief roots twenty feet deep
losing green fingers one-by-one
to count the weeks after new year

till splayed leaf hands turn to bone.

never going to heaven

time eludes us as it bothers others
instead deceives loneliness

shadow's shadow glows with life
sodium & ruby light like dungeness

on a humming night popping shots
a rattling rattle in dark doorways

like dungeness two-by-two
sunshine frames through the cottage

stinking hawksbeard floating on passion
lying dead still asking if we cruise

in a beige suit or shy away
like a jay in a blue flash

dear derek jarman

i've built a garden somewhere
but you did it nowhere. you said
my garden's boundaries are the horizon
you didn't only mean dungeness
when you said *there are no walls or fences*
you weren't describing our inward journey
or casting a shadow across the floor
of *heaven*. since you made those films
you don't know rivulets run through
my parched grass. as if being banned
and disliked is a pinnacle after all.

you refused to die without the sun
rising without stones threaded
and hung in a garden that grew out
of nothing, without going quietly
smiling in slow motion like an iceberg
sinking from the sky, the ripples still
licking shingle in a one-way tide.

when i visit prospect cottage

i'll take you five dried yellow roses
(one fell apart) i'll repaint the wall
on the side with *The Sunne Rising*
blame black tar for making me
then forget what it was i came here
to escape

wild rabbits

five lighthouses

Between
1615 and 1961,
Dungeness had
five lighthouses built
farther and
farther
east.

The first one to be built was rudimentary
a treehouse where I used open fires for
my light and the carpets didn't help.

A hundred-foot tower made of bricks
seemed an extreme response, but I was
a teenager.

This lighthouse was neither noticed nor
noticing so I built another closer to a disco.

It had seventeen argon lights, a glitter ball
in the sky, which worked best when it
was raining men.

My fourth footprint had seven floors in ironic
black & white, impregnated
concrete rings with a veranda

more than anyone could ever want
the lights were fired by my arms & liver
and little dried chunks of my soul.

The slowness of shingle banks shifting my
eyes until it was too late. When all I could see
was river & silt

my lighthouse was only how it looked. Then
towards water again I placed another in a
garden of railway sleepers

hag stones and a home-made compost
heap, where the sea recedes still towards its
inevitable oneness

even though it already has.

my walls are made of bungaroosh

lots of soft stuff, agèd lime flaking
but also half bricks, cobblestones
in-between pebbles, broken shells
& coral, which just goes to show
we all have a bit of sea inside us.
Of course, there's flint that could
start a fire, be a weapon or a tool.
The walls of my home are the same
inside & out — hidden by stuccoed
façades. But my walled garden is
unabashed & naked to the eye —
— shuttering formed the four walls
excluding those who believe it
is the worst material in the world.

back to the soil

Dipping hands in every now & then swapping white roses & chrysanths for black crescent nails in a to & fro with the fingers. I used to want to drown my smell in a car or hang my taste in a garage, but now desire is daffodils & fuchsia. My gardening riddles my fate in practice-runs of bonfire ashes & rotting *what-was-once-useful* in a wooden box. In the meantime, foxglove & lily-of-the-valley are my closest brushes with death. Inside these four-walls of bright & shade, shifting as the day edges by & seasons creep to where, we cannot tell.

according to martin

i love to sit on that garden bench
the one made from recycled cartwheels
the way i feel about myself
how i wonder about my sibling
sculpted from rock
i blend camaraderie & outrage
like starlings & squirrels
though both are fringed
with grey & regret
the way basil turns bitter-sweet
if cut by a knife
how sometimes sweetness can only be smelt
by ripping things apart
how often i'm torn between
tongue & belly
pink & blue textures
ice cream & cum
the way a spider spins silk & eats its prey
he loves to imagine
what lies beneath it & who i am
playing in this drama singing what

i've got this gut feeling that inside somewhere

there is this hairy creature, a fenodyree
busy naked with its chores
a nimble mower of rough hedges
shouldering stones one way or another
with a melancholic wail when my body
crumbles like a tholtan, maybe it is released
from its unchosen home to herd loaghtan sheep
on foggy nights.

Perhaps it's a buggane, a huge hairier ogre
ripping the roof off Sunday School beliefs
a bull with tusks glistening red eyes torched
with rum until I'm gone when it shape-shifts
out of my form into silver snauanee
into ferrish mist.

the naughty corner

in the far diagonal of my garden
where all the veg off-cuts are confined
two bins rot along with pruned plants
feeding slugs & snails. The self-made
planter from a dead lilac, two old pallets &
assorted branches frame two gnomes —
obviously cloned — but no faeries are to be seen.

The fenodyree & ferrishyn have *Beware!*
signs of their own in English.
I would if I were you. Belief that some
things don't exist doesn't mean
they don't make a difference. Ask Jesus.
More languages have died than been born.
If they were never written down, did they
ever even exist?
Yn Ghaelg is a Lazarus but I still can't find
proper warning signs:

Bee-jee er nyn dwooaie fenodyree!
Bee-jee er nyn dwooaie ferrishyn!
Yn corneil olkyssagh

square walled garden

A sparrowhawk circles & hovers above
the dead fortune apple festooned with bird feeders.
Is a tree really dead if you can hear
it serving a purpose?

A skeletal fig sprouts tiny green buds & leaves
an avocado cowering below the cherry blossom.
Neither will fruit — unlike the fig in its next life.

A stylish window grille hangs on one wall along-
side a seatless metal chair — *raison d'être perdue.*
Art & beauty extend beyond
the confines of utility.

The hawk's flight now a tightening screw, twisted
hazel, red dogwood, bay in talons' reach, a Manx
flag with three flapping legs. Oh... and a pigeon.

goldfinches

Painted beauties visit both our gardens.
Rob offers them sunflower seeds, eagerly
pecked, mine only devour nyger, in spite
of being given the two — I wonder
whether they are settling for second best
or if they are just happy to accept whatever
is on offer — maybe these dead seeds are
an acquired taste like sweetbreads. Like me.

The finch's markings bewitch me for all their
twitchy suspicion. Glad Rob's not like that
apart from the colours of his kindness. Now
I know they prefer teasel & thistle, I never
thought I'd say *at my age accept what you can.*

for Robert Hamberger

the first rule of bird-spotting

After seven days on safari, Father
scored one hundred and nine, with me
behind on ninety-nine, perhaps because
I was late to what was really going on.

To be certain about anything, we rely
on colours, spots, stripes or bands,
the hood-eared, bearded or crest & tail,
the shape of its beak, coverts & flanks

including *what-can-only-be-seen-in-flight.*
How it might not be the place you'd expect
to find it. This requires patience, quiet,
some might say love — but that would mean

every thing is a bird with feathers, even guilt
about the great spotted woodpecker
on my Flower Power balls, how I didn't know
their gender or full name.

narcissus pseudonarcissus

We all inhabit a relationship with something — for me
it is firm stems springing from fleshy globules, heads
that tilt in a breath. My tastes vary like my desires —

for example, *Narcissus W. P. Milner* is simple
yet handsome with silver skin and its miniature
trumpet, though I prefer the much taller *martinette* —

whose tolerance is broad, its multi-headed arched neck
swaying — like a bent gangster overlooks their street.
I yearn for *Narcissus poeticus* buried six inches deep

in my perennial border — that pheasant eye red-ringed
as a rusty sheriff's badge swinging in the shade
of his rimmed hat — starfruit with a creamy fringe.

Who would have thought that *Narcissus poeticus*
would fail to blossom, leave me flopping, green.

the third side of a coin

is on the edge — the truth
doesn't land easily unless thrown
into cold custard or warm mash —
comfort & discomfort sharing
a bed. I remember those days
when I tossed & turned, also
turned & tossed, slept on the edge —
heads & tails refused to speak
in fact, the head tried to eat the tail
& the tail had a crack at thinking
all by itself — with predictable
outcomes. I've been rolling
ever since.

dead rabbits

despite all available evidence

I know more about building sand
dams than a sane person would want
mainly because I had my leg broken
on purpose, that said, I am mostly
Irish & Manx-blooded after I killed
my brother in my sleep
I missed his funeral after having
been elected to high office.

I have a firm grip on my Tuesday scarf
handmade by Tom D Slaughter
which reminds me I know too much
about children dying in cricket scores
by reading cover-to-cover *Wisden*
and *Dialogue on Diarrhoea*. Talking
saves more lives than drones.

a walk with federico garcía lorca

i

the sky is grey with every type of shadow
so complex it forms a new constellation
self-named Stegosaurus Major.

under a force from itself the moon retires
the spring tides on overtime strike leave
beaches awash with human detritus.

orphaned teenagers know the difference
between their mothers' flotsam & jetsam.
for sure, deaf children can still hear drones

bombs don't drop accidentally from the sky
like starlings or yellow-headed blackbirds.
the little animals whose skulls are cracked.

ii

a butterfly drowned in the inkwell
a lizard crawls down a throat
platefuls of stomach
bobbing in the Atlantic
a wet-sponge dummy
wrung until wet
dressed in rags, but with dry feet
crumbling stone, crumbs for rats,
worm tapas, dust where angels fled
tastes like…what? no, not likely
anyway, watching Siamese twins
howling, orcas eating the tongue
of a humpback calf, and we have
a primetime view, bobbing in
a bath, considering the options.

iii

a crocodile breaks a muddy surface
the herd of ghost zebra disappears.
does the wildebeest think twice
before it crosses a river?
like warthogs back into waterholes
balancing thirst & survival?

what's the difference
between the real meaning
of ambivalence and certainty?

why do fallen stars flash silver & gold
when pavements shimmer with rain & oil
reflecting rainbows *cut down by the sky?*

rather than undertake a new epic

birds eat each other whole then open
a shop called *Beak to Tail* in Hackney.
A browser asks — *how does it taste?*

Christmas dinner is an oxymoron.
Jesus roasts parsnips over charcoal
smoke reflects in a misty-eyed omen.

Angels know who they are. The Devil
is a fiction made real by repetition
Defence! Defence! Defence!

The opposite of epic could be tragic.
Disguising yourself as a metal bird
doesn't make it any less of a crime.

acceptable loss

So long as an underlying health condition
isn't recurrent herpes or persistent cystitis
I guess the old will die anyway
just as we will
    & the family will inherit what's left.

In 2030, a WHO delegation fly business class
to a grave in Eswatini and eloquently state this
year's four hundred-thousandth AIDS death marks
an acceptable loss
    & the family will give them tea.

So long as an underlying cause of the condition
isn't genocide or a US invasion for the greater good
I guess the young will die anyway
just as we will
    & their sibling will inherit the gun.

It's 2020, and the plumber asks me
how much the tap is leaking
I say *about one Kenyan family a day* — he says it is
an acceptable loss
    & we play Snakes & Ladders with a loaded die.

fuchsia as in future

God's Tears in Manx Gaelic metaphor
unlike the Catholic Blood of Christ
the weep of Pope Francis every night

for Gaza, there are F-fighters
showering shrapnel not flowers
bodies petalled in red & purple

'fū' as in glad it's not me
'shə' as in don't mention it
might jeopardise your career

'p-ər' as in the Press, like stigmata
the sins of omission, literally
holes in your soles

'fē' as in phenomenal feat
to see through our hands
to forget, as in forsake

blue-ringed octopus

anthropomorphism:
the inability of humans to judge the behaviour of another
species outside of their norms or beyond their intelligence.

When provoked, this octopus turns bright yellow
with glowing blue rings. Humans find this attractive

— they are only human after all — so much so in fact
they ~~harvest~~ take them from ~~the wild~~ non-protected areas.

Apparently they don't travel well, and often escape tanks.
Experts don't recommend as pets because of their bite.

A blue-ringed octopus has three times the neural wiring
capacity of humans — but octopus arms also interact with

their environment with minimal input from their brain.
They are seemingly mild-mannered, introverted animals

except, presumably, when they hunt, paralyse, crunch and
eat their prey. *However, they are more sociable on MDMA.*

What is written focuses chiefly on the octopus venom
— *its bite is enough to kill twenty-six people within minutes.*

Reportedly there have only ever been sixteen people dead.
Humans say they are the most poisonous creatures on earth.

dear humanity

Violet is red withdrawn from humanity by blue
—Wassily Kandinsky

Some things keep me awake at night. Almost
every piece of advice says tell them like it is.
So here goes. I don't know you anymore.
Inside we are *white — a harmony of silence*
shrouds life from our understanding. Serpents
feed off fear shaped by generational memory.

I've come to realise you ~~don't count the dead~~
question how many people really die from that
choose not to count all those lives left in ruins
the second antithesis between white and black
— a silence devoid of possibilities, perhaps why
too many children say they'd prefer death to this.

It's as if every mirror on Earth has been shattered
though I looked at you last week and saw myself
black — motionless like ashes of a funeral pyre.
It's hard to watch a child about to take that breath
consider thousands of them to be our kith & kin
but can you imagine just one as your own son?

Language is supposed to be my thing, so I notice
when a sentence doesn't have a subject or object
and different verbs depending on colour & creed.
Orange is red brought nearer to you by yellow.
If, whilst held captive, a snake eats its own tail
it has mistaken itself as either predator or prey.

the world is hell, and men are both

though they ought not to be
    in this world, as it ought to be
with those devils nurtured inside
    the tormented souls are animals

    animals the tormented souls
they chop up — male chicks
    they won't breed — bull calves
won't eat grass — the ram lambs
    circle & circle — the fish
sleep horizontal — the trees

    crumble — the icebergs
so hidden-assed & wet eye-lashed — men
    without knowing, this thing-within
is a thing-in-itself — unknowable but felt.

after Arthur Schopenhauer

forest fire

I want you to act as if our house is on fire. Because it is.
—Greta Thunberg

Pencil and Aleppo pines migrated to the Holy Land
from Europe, carefully naturalised amongst the last
remnants of villages, Bedouin camps.

Native olives bulldozed — uprooted well before their prime.
Eucalyptus drained the swamps, sucking water
from great depths.

It then spread wider, grew fast, starved
what lies beneath — ruined lands so well-covered
even if cyclamens survive with the dead

needles and dried leaves until those blazes break out
in barren soils. Fire breeds fire, villages burn again
in biblical proportions —

scientists say it's common for invasive species
especially in a tinderbox.

to hope

after Jane Hirshfield

You ruin a life
as a worm eats an apple
inside out, lays its eggs
for future generations.
But you are not a worm
nor a lamp, nor a religion.
For some you are never there
like a white Christmas
or a roof over the head
its skylight view of stars, and planets
like Pluto that lost its designation
had to settle for less.
A lamp, the easy obedience
of a switch
except when filaments spark & snap.
According to the Quran a stone split
open for you — a spring
replenished by seasonal rain
feeding more than you can eat.
You teach us there is an after-life
even if it's not worth living, again.

It's not the despair, Laura.
I can stand the despair.
It's the hope…

Abstract nouns have their own life
whether we want it or not
a mosquito can't resist a lamp,
zebras depend on their stripes,
mosquitoes on the face of a Jain.
You are the same smell
as napalm in the morning
but only if we can smell it.
And if a small tear swells
in the corner of one eye, it is you
in all your brutality.
I have seen you beat a man
until he weeps like a converted soul.
You are that cat only wanting to play
but I admire the mouse
running under the fridge.

mouse run

It's as if a mouse is hiding — in wait every day
for me to do the gardening — then jumps nine
steps, vaulting the door frame into the kitchen.
On those nights, I catch one in a humane trap.
This must be a coincidence, but it is not
the same mouse — except for that time
I carried one to the compost heap for a treat
which it clearly regarded as a day-excursion.

Now I take them away to *World Peace Gardens*
in the hope — up the road — they find solace
perhaps even a greater sense of purpose
than the creamed hazelnut mix at the end
of a plastic tunnel. Maybe this is what's meant
by a humane trap — making the same mistakes
with refined effort. That much I know
having trampled those criss-crossed paths
filled with plenty — of sex, drugs & ice cream.

Every time I tend my garden, I juggle with
death in search of bread, perhaps
like the mouse, or maybe mice prefer to eat
the hearts of seeds, leaving husks like skeletons
for pigeons to pick over. I prefer different avian
visitors, even yearn for flashes of jay & a robin
to bring back my dead, remind me to live outside
a plastic tunnel, watching nature pass me by.

turned upside-down

using slates from the roof
bring my seventies stone patio
up to a retro state of shattered

at times we need to take down
layered tiles that shield us —
smash into unavoidable pieces

slated fragments fill my paths
the cracks help the storms seep
in a good way, like plants root

i sit on the old cartwheel bench —
my broken remains, listen to wrens
and robins instead of facing all that

common gull shit, i smell compost
— scent hyacinths in sky

life is there, above the walls

after Paul Verlaine

the iron stairway is filled
with lavender and mint.
A flag is, above the walls,
a symbol of wind and rebirth.

The rooftops across
squawking tiles and chimney pots,
common gulls plotting their forays
above the sea, the world is —

pigeons roosting amongst the figs
like flying squirrels without teeth,
life is there, above the walls,
but quietly murmurs here —

what will you do, below there,
dreaming without pauses,
say, what will you do, below there,
with your choices?

notes

The poem appearing as an epigraph is inspired by Kay Ryan's 'Carrying a Ladder'.

'[gripped]' and 'the boy [erased]' are erasure poems from *Queerfella* (The Rialto, 2020).

'nature poem' is inspired by Danez Smith's 'fall poem'.

'according to locals' — mwethya is the Kamba tribe's concept of community self-help in Kenya.

'according to the signs': Manx Gaelic: Raad ny Foillan is literally 'The Way of the Gull' the name for the Isle of Man coastal path.

Gob ny Rona is literally Point of the Seals, a headland between Port y Vullen and Port Lewaigue.

'a golden wedding' is a Golden Shovel from Essex Hemphill's 'American Wedding'.

'good friday' is inspired by an old Manx custom on Good Friday [Jeheiney Caisht] of a Flitter Daunsey [Flitter Dance]. Manx Gaelic: flitter - limpet / soddag - thick cake / crosh - cross / cuirn - rowan / shligganyn - shells.

'one size fits all' was the strapline of the club XXL. 'sequins /... / hiding a speck of darkness / overcome' is a play on Caroline Bird's Carcanet Blog, 27 February 2019, 'as if every sequin represents a tiny speck of darkness overcome'.

'stigma' uses found words from Derek Jarman.

'life confirmed as a time bomb': The right-hand column is found words from Derek Jarman.

'famous for fairlight donkeys': a local nickname for rabbits, as told to Neil Bartlett by Keith Collins. The B&Q comment is also Neil's.

'after the bluebells turned to concrete' is inspired by Tilda Swinton (*Derek Jarman's Modern Nature*, John Hansard Gallery, 2021).

'i could have been you': The character Ritchie Tozer in the drama *It's A Sin* was inspired by the actor, dancer and singer Dursley McLinden, born in Douglas, Isle of Man, May 1965.

'a manx politician walks into a mirrored room'. The Department of Health and Manx Care says it doesn't know how many HIV cases there are on the Isle of Man and has no plans to publish HIV statistics, claiming it could lead to patients being identified (Manx Radio, 12th June 2013 and 3FM, 14th March 2022).

'i've got this gut feeling that inside somewhere' is from Maurice Riordan's 'The Jailbird'. Manx Gaelic: tholtan - ruined cottage / snauanee - web-like covering of the ground on a dewy dawn / ferrish - faerie.

'the naughty corner' — Yn Ghaelg - Manx Gaelic / Bee-jee er nyn dwooaie! - Beware! / fenodyree - gnome-like creatures / ferrishyn - fairies / yn corneil olkyssagh - the naughty corner.

'*rather than undertake a new epic*' is from John Ashbery's 'Hotel Lautréamont'.

'a walk with federico garcía lorca': The poems use four lines from Lorca's 'After a Walk'.

'blue-ringed octopus': the anthropomorphism 'definition' is the author's own.

'to hope': 'It's not the despair, Laura. I can stand the despair. It's the hope…' is from the film, *Clockwise* (Michael Frayn, 1986).

'life is there, above the walls' is from Paul Verlaine's poem 'The Sky Above the Roof'.

acknowledgements

I am immensely grateful to the following for their financial support during the writing of this book: Arts Council England, Culture Vannin, Grand Camp Maisie Fund, Royal Literary Fund, and Society of Authors.

I am indebted to Arvon, Creative Future, New Writing South, Poetry School and The Literary Consultancy for their bursaries and concessionary rates since 2018, including two 'TLC Free Reads' from Ahren Warner (2022) and Simon Barraclough (2024).

With thanks to the publishers and editors of the following pamphlets, who published poems (or previous versions of them) in this collection.

Pamphlets

Throatbone, Uncollected Press, 2020 – 'lamping wild rabbits'.
Isle of Sin, Polari Press, 2023 – 'i could have been you', 'a manx politician walks into a mirrored room'.
The Whole Island, Valley Press, 2023 – 'our language drips', 'according to the signs'.
a finger in derek jarman's mouth, Polari Press, 2024 – 'HIV stigma', 'life confirmed as a time bomb', 'dungeness', 'powered by HIV', 'famous for fairlight donkeys', 'after the bluebells turned to concrete', 'the visitors', 'crambe maritima', 'never going to heaven' 'dear derek jarman', 'when I visit prospect cottage'.

Also, thanks to the following anthology and magazine publishers.

Anthologies

Broken Sleep Books, Fawn Press, Hammond House Publishing, John Hansard Gallery, Nine Pens Press, Propel Magazine, Sídhe Press, The Broken Spine, The Winchester Poetry Prize.

Magazines and Websites

& Change, *Abridged*, *Ambient Receiver*, *Ambit Magazine*, *Amethyst Review*, *DREICH*, *Finished Creatures*, *Gutter*, *HIV Here & Now*, *Impossible Archetype Journal*, *Long Poem Magazine*, *Lighthouse Journal*, *Manx Reflections*, *MODRON*, *Poetry Wales*, *Poetry Worth Hearing*, *Propel Magazine*, *Southword*, *Stand*, *Stone of Madness*, *t'ART*, *The Aftershock Review*, *The Alchemy Spoon*, *The Four Faced Liar*, *The Frogmore Papers*, *The Rialto*, *The Write Launch*, *Under the Radar*.

thanks

Heartfelt thanks to Anthony Anaxagorou and Patricia Ferguson for co-parenting my debut collection with such love & professionalism. I am indebted to Anthony, who was the first poet & teacher to encourage & mentor me when I started out in 2018. Alongside Joelle Taylor, another early teacher & mentor, Anthony & Out-Spoken remain a constant inspiration.

It would be remiss not to acknowledge the other fantastic teachers I have had, most especially Rachael Allen, Maurice Riordan, Richard Scott, Wayne Holloway-Smith & Jack Underwood.

Thanks to Naomi Foyle & Rob Hamberger for their support, encouragement & editorial feedback for my original submitted manuscript, whose belief in me was matched by my other dear friend, alice hiller.

Thanks to past and present members of The Crocodile Collective (Vasiliki Albedo, Nóra Blascsók, Rowan Lyster, Mary Mulholland & Julie Runacres) for their friendship & feedback on many of these poems. Thanks also to all the Poetry Society Stanza poets who gave individual poem feedback: Brighton, Covent Garden, SKEGS. Gura mie ayd to Ruth Keggin Gell from Culture Vannin for the help with the Yn Ghaelg.

Immeasurable thanks also to all the friends & family who have supported me unconditionally in yet another radical departure from a previous life.

Dedicated to (Kathleen Patricia) Penny Maddrell (1931-2008).